S0-AUX-886

QUILT
ADDRESS BOOK

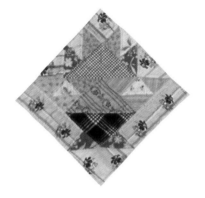

A Sterling/Museum Quilts Book
Sterling Publishing Co., Inc.   New York

The quilts featured in this address book are from the
Susan Jenkins Collection

A B
CACTUS QUILT Pennsylvania c. 1900

C D
BOW-TIE c.1930

E F
LOG CABIN c.1880

G H
CRAZY QUILT c.1890

I J K
MENNONITE BOW-TIE Ohio c.1920

L M
SCHOOLHOUSE Oklahoma c.1940

N O
TREE OF LIFE North Carolina 1911

P Q
REVERSE APPLIQUE Vermont c.1870

R S
AMISH CACTUS BASKET Ohio c.1930

T U
MENNONITE DOUBLE IRISH CHAIN Pennsylvania c.1900

V W
FOLK ART APPLIQUE Pennsylvania c.1860

X Y Z
DRESDEN PLATE c.1900

Published by Sterling Publishing Company, Inc.
387 Park Avenue South, New York, NY 10016
And by Museum Quilts Publications
254-258 Goswell Road, London EC1V 7EB
Distributed in Canada by Sterling Publishing
c/o Canadian Manda Group, P.O. Box 920, Station U
Toronto, Ontario, Canada M8Z 5P9
Distributed in Australia by Capricorn Link Ltd.
P.O. Box 665 Lane Cove, NSW 2066

Copyright © 1993 by Museum Quilts Publications

All rights reserved. No part of this publication may be reproduced or transmitted
in any form or by any means, electronic or mechanical, including photocopy, recording,
or any information storage and retrieval system now known or to be invented
without permission in writing from the publishers

Design by Bet Ayer

Printed and bound in Korea

ISBN: 1 897954 01 8

NAME

ADDRESS

☎ HOME   ☎ WORK

FAX   BIRTHDAY

NAME

ADDRESS

☎ HOME   ☎ WORK

FAX   BIRTHDAY

NAME

ADDRESS

☎ HOME   ☎ WORK

FAX   BIRTHDAY

NAME

ADDRESS

☎ HOME   ☎ WORK

FAX   BIRTHDAY

NAME

ADDRESS

☎ HOME   ☎ WORK

FAX   BIRTHDAY

NAME	
ADDRESS	
☎ HOME	☎ WORK
FAX	BIRTHDAY
NAME	
ADDRESS	
☎ HOME	☎ WORK
FAX	BIRTHDAY
NAME	
ADDRESS	
☎ HOME	☎ WORK
FAX	BIRTHDAY
NAME	
ADDRESS	
☎ HOME	☎ WORK
FAX	BIRTHDAY
NAME	
ADDRESS	
☎ HOME	☎ WORK
FAX	BIRTHDAY

NAME

ADDRESS

☎ HOME   ☎ WORK

FAX   BIRTHDAY

NAME

ADDRESS

☎ HOME   ☎ WORK

FAX   BIRTHDAY

NAME

ADDRESS

☎ HOME   ☎ WORK

FAX   BIRTHDAY

NAME

ADDRESS

☎ HOME   ☎ WORK

FAX   BIRTHDAY

NAME

ADDRESS

☎ HOME   ☎ WORK

FAX   BIRTHDAY

NAME

ADDRESS

☎ HOME   ☎ WORK

FAX   BIRTHDAY

NAME

ADDRESS

☎ HOME   ☎ WORK

FAX   BIRTHDAY

NAME

ADDRESS

☎ HOME   ☎ WORK

FAX   BIRTHDAY

NAME

ADDRESS

☎ HOME   ☎ WORK

FAX   BIRTHDAY

NAME

ADDRESS

☎ HOME   ☎ WORK

FAX   BIRTHDAY

NAME

ADDRESS

☎ HOME   ☎ WORK

FAX   BIRTHDAY

NAME

ADDRESS

☎ HOME   ☎ WORK

FAX   BIRTHDAY

NAME

ADDRESS

☎ HOME   ☎ WORK

FAX   BIRTHDAY

NAME

ADDRESS

☎ HOME   ☎ WORK

FAX   BIRTHDAY

NAME

ADDRESS

☎ HOME   ☎ WORK

FAX   BIRTHDAY

NAME

ADDRESS

☎ HOME   ☎ WORK

FAX   BIRTHDAY

NAME

ADDRESS

☎ HOME   ☎ WORK

FAX   BIRTHDAY

NAME

ADDRESS

☎ HOME   ☎ WORK

FAX   BIRTHDAY

NAME

ADDRESS

☎ HOME   ☎ WORK

FAX   BIRTHDAY

NAME

ADDRESS

☎ HOME   ☎ WORK

FAX   BIRTHDAY

NAME

ADDRESS

☎ HOME   ☎ WORK

FAX   BIRTHDAY

NAME

ADDRESS

☎ HOME   ☎ WORK

FAX   BIRTHDAY

NAME

ADDRESS

☎ HOME   ☎ WORK

FAX   BIRTHDAY

NAME

ADDRESS

☎ HOME   ☎ WORK

FAX   BIRTHDAY

NAME

ADDRESS

☎ HOME   ☎ WORK

FAX   BIRTHDAY

NAME

ADDRESS

☎ HOME   ☎ WORK

FAX   BIRTHDAY

NAME

ADDRESS

☎ HOME   ☎ WORK

FAX   BIRTHDAY

NAME

ADDRESS

☎ HOME   ☎ WORK

FAX   BIRTHDAY

NAME

ADDRESS

☎ HOME   ☎ WORK

FAX   BIRTHDAY

NAME

ADDRESS

☎ HOME   ☎ WORK

FAX   BIRTHDAY

NAME

ADDRESS

☎ HOME   ☎ WORK

FAX   BIRTHDAY

NAME

ADDRESS

☎ HOME   ☎ WORK

FAX   BIRTHDAY

NAME

ADDRESS

☎ HOME   ☎ WORK

FAX   BIRTHDAY

NAME

ADDRESS

☎ HOME   ☎ WORK

FAX   BIRTHDAY

NAME

ADDRESS

☎ HOME   ☎ WORK

FAX   BIRTHDAY

NAME

ADDRESS

☎ HOME   ☎ WORK

FAX   BIRTHDAY

NAME

ADDRESS

☎ HOME   ☎ WORK

FAX   BIRTHDAY

NAME

ADDRESS

☎ HOME   ☎ WORK

FAX   BIRTHDAY

NAME

ADDRESS

☎ HOME   ☎ WORK

FAX   BIRTHDAY

NAME

ADDRESS

☎ HOME   ☎ WORK

FAX   BIRTHDAY

NAME

ADDRESS

☎ HOME   ☎ WORK

FAX   BIRTHDAY

NAME

ADDRESS

☎ HOME   ☎ WORK

FAX   BIRTHDAY

NAME

ADDRESS

☎ HOME   ☎ WORK

FAX   BIRTHDAY

NAME

ADDRESS

☎ HOME   ☎ WORK

FAX   BIRTHDAY

NAME

ADDRESS

☎ HOME   ☎ WORK

FAX   BIRTHDAY

NAME

ADDRESS

☎ HOME   ☎ WORK

FAX   BIRTHDAY

NAME

ADDRESS

☎ HOME   ☎ WORK

FAX   BIRTHDAY

NAME

ADDRESS

☎ HOME   ☎ WORK

FAX   BIRTHDAY

NAME

ADDRESS

☎ HOME   ☎ WORK

FAX   BIRTHDAY

NAME

ADDRESS

☎ HOME   ☎ WORK

FAX   BIRTHDAY

NAME

ADDRESS

☎ HOME   ☎ WORK

FAX   BIRTHDAY

NAME

ADDRESS

☎ HOME   ☎ WORK

FAX   BIRTHDAY

NAME

ADDRESS

☎ HOME   ☎ WORK

FAX   BIRTHDAY

NAME

ADDRESS

☎ HOME   ☎ WORK

FAX   BIRTHDAY

NAME

ADDRESS

☎ HOME   ☎ WORK

FAX   BIRTHDAY

NAME

ADDRESS

☎ HOME   ☎ WORK

FAX   BIRTHDAY

NAME

ADDRESS

☎ HOME   ☎ WORK

FAX   BIRTHDAY

NAME

ADDRESS

☎ HOME   ☎ WORK

FAX   BIRTHDAY

NAME

ADDRESS

☎ HOME   ☎ WORK

FAX   BIRTHDAY

NAME

ADDRESS

☎ HOME   ☎ WORK

FAX   BIRTHDAY

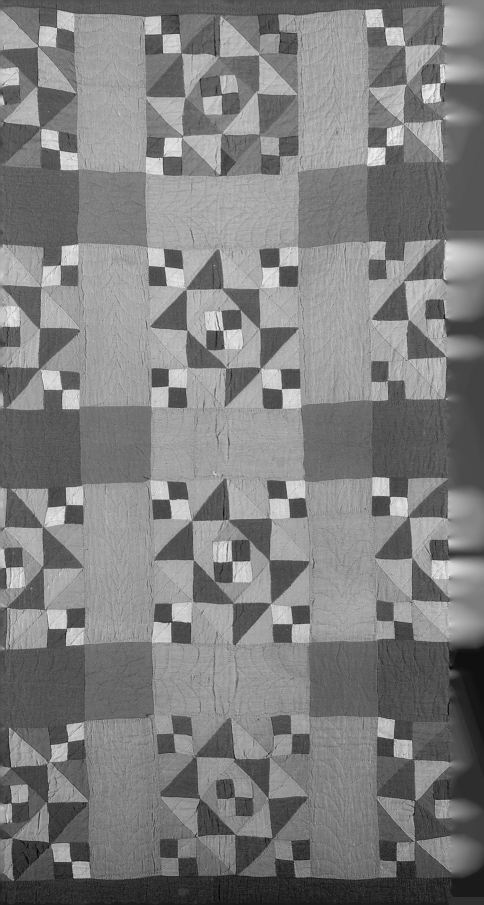

NAME

ADDRESS

☎ HOME   ☎ WORK

FAX   BIRTHDAY

NAME

ADDRESS

☎ HOME   ☎ WORK

FAX   BIRTHDAY

NAME

ADDRESS

☎ HOME   ☎ WORK

FAX   BIRTHDAY

NAME

ADDRESS

☎ HOME   ☎ WORK

FAX   BIRTHDAY

NAME

ADDRESS

☎ HOME   ☎ WORK

FAX   BIRTHDAY

NAME

ADDRESS

☎ HOME   ☎ WORK

FAX   BIRTHDAY

NAME

ADDRESS

☎ HOME   ☎ WORK

FAX   BIRTHDAY

NAME

ADDRESS

☎ HOME   ☎ WORK

FAX   BIRTHDAY

NAME

ADDRESS

☎ HOME   ☎ WORK

FAX   BIRTHDAY

NAME

ADDRESS

☎ HOME   ☎ WORK

FAX   BIRTHDAY

NAME

ADDRESS

☎ HOME   ☎ WORK

FAX   BIRTHDAY

NAME

ADDRESS

☎ HOME   ☎ WORK

FAX   BIRTHDAY

NAME

ADDRESS

☎ HOME   ☎ WORK

FAX   BIRTHDAY

NAME

ADDRESS

☎ HOME   ☎ WORK

FAX   BIRTHDAY

NAME

ADDRESS

☎ HOME   ☎ WORK

FAX   BIRTHDAY

NAME

ADDRESS

☎ HOME   ☎ WORK

FAX   BIRTHDAY

NAME

ADDRESS

☎ HOME   ☎ WORK

FAX   BIRTHDAY

NAME

ADDRESS

☎ HOME   ☎ WORK

FAX   BIRTHDAY

NAME

ADDRESS

☎ HOME   ☎ WORK

FAX   BIRTHDAY

NAME

ADDRESS

☎ HOME   ☎ WORK

FAX   BIRTHDAY

NAME

ADDRESS

☎ HOME   ☎ WORK

FAX   BIRTHDAY

NAME

ADDRESS

☎ HOME   ☎ WORK

FAX   BIRTHDAY

NAME

ADDRESS

☎ HOME   ☎ WORK

FAX   BIRTHDAY

NAME

ADDRESS

☎ HOME   ☎ WORK

FAX   BIRTHDAY

NAME

ADDRESS

☎ HOME   ☎ WORK

FAX   BIRTHDAY

NAME

ADDRESS

☎ HOME   ☎ WORK

FAX   BIRTHDAY

NAME

ADDRESS

☎ HOME   ☎ WORK

FAX   BIRTHDAY

NAME

ADDRESS

☎ HOME   ☎ WORK

FAX   BIRTHDAY

NAME

ADDRESS

☎ HOME   ☎ WORK

FAX   BIRTHDAY

NAME

ADDRESS

☎ HOME   ☎ WORK

FAX   BIRTHDAY

NAME

ADDRESS

☎ HOME   ☎ WORK

FAX   BIRTHDAY

NAME

ADDRESS

☎ HOME   ☎ WORK

FAX   BIRTHDAY

NAME

ADDRESS

☎ HOME   ☎ WORK

FAX   BIRTHDAY

NAME

ADDRESS

☎ HOME   ☎ WORK

FAX   BIRTHDAY

NAME

ADDRESS

☎ HOME   ☎ WORK

FAX   BIRTHDAY

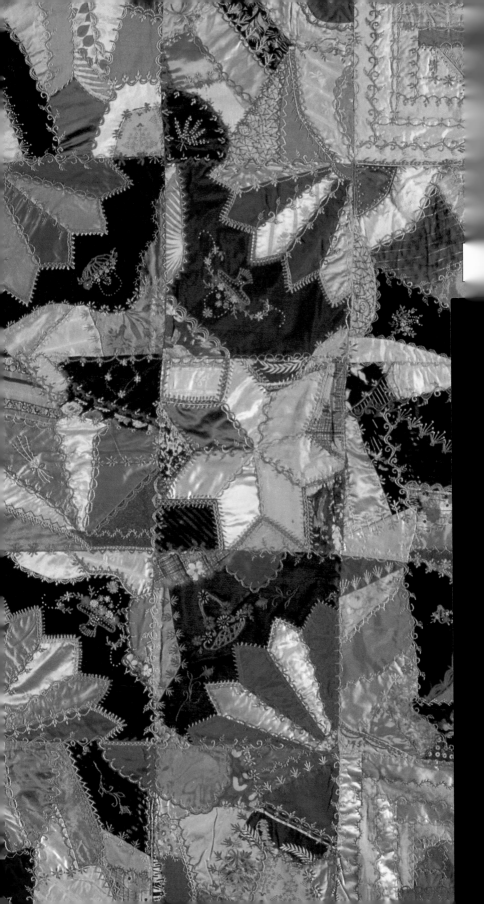

NAME

ADDRESS

☎ HOME   ☎ WORK

FAX   BIRTHDAY

NAME

ADDRESS

☎ HOME   ☎ WORK

FAX   BIRTHDAY

NAME

ADDRESS

☎ HOME   ☎ WORK

FAX   BIRTHDAY

NAME

ADDRESS

☎ HOME   ☎ WORK

FAX   BIRTHDAY

NAME

ADDRESS

☎ HOME   ☎ WORK

FAX   BIRTHDAY

NAME

ADDRESS

☎ HOME   ☎ WORK

FAX   BIRTHDAY

NAME

ADDRESS

☎ HOME   ☎ WORK

FAX   BIRTHDAY

NAME

ADDRESS

☎ HOME   ☎ WORK

FAX   BIRTHDAY

NAME

ADDRESS

☎ HOME   ☎ WORK

FAX   BIRTHDAY

NAME

ADDRESS

☎ HOME   ☎ WORK

FAX   BIRTHDAY

NAME	
ADDRESS	
☎ HOME	☎ WORK
FAX	BIRTHDAY
NAME	
ADDRESS	
☎ HOME	☎ WORK
FAX	BIRTHDAY
NAME	
ADDRESS	
☎ HOME	☎ WORK
FAX	BIRTHDAY
NAME	
ADDRESS	
☎ HOME	☎ WORK
FAX	BIRTHDAY
NAME	
ADDRESS	
☎ HOME	☎ WORK
FAX	BIRTHDAY

NAME

ADDRESS

☎ HOME   ☎ WORK

FAX   BIRTHDAY

NAME

ADDRESS

☎ HOME   ☎ WORK

FAX   BIRTHDAY

NAME

ADDRESS

☎ HOME   ☎ WORK

FAX   BIRTHDAY

NAME

ADDRESS

☎ HOME   ☎ WORK

FAX   BIRTHDAY

NAME

ADDRESS

☎ HOME   ☎ WORK

FAX   BIRTHDAY

NAME	
ADDRESS	
☎ HOME	☎ WORK
FAX	BIRTHDAY
NAME	
ADDRESS	
☎ HOME	☎ WORK
FAX	BIRTHDAY
NAME	
ADDRESS	
☎ HOME	☎ WORK
FAX	BIRTHDAY
NAME	
ADDRESS	
☎ HOME	☎ WORK
FAX	BIRTHDAY
NAME	
ADDRESS	
☎ HOME	☎ WORK
FAX	BIRTHDAY

NAME

ADDRESS

☎ HOME   ☎ WORK

FAX   BIRTHDAY

NAME

ADDRESS

☎ HOME   ☎ WORK

FAX   BIRTHDAY

NAME

ADDRESS

☎ HOME   ☎ WORK

FAX   BIRTHDAY

NAME

ADDRESS

☎ HOME   ☎ WORK

FAX   BIRTHDAY

NAME

ADDRESS

☎ HOME   ☎ WORK

FAX   BIRTHDAY

NAME

ADDRESS

☎ HOME   ☎ WORK

FAX   BIRTHDAY

NAME

ADDRESS

☎ HOME   ☎ WORK

FAX   BIRTHDAY

NAME

ADDRESS

☎ HOME   ☎ WORK

FAX   BIRTHDAY

NAME

ADDRESS

☎ HOME   ☎ WORK

FAX   BIRTHDAY

NAME

ADDRESS

☎ HOME   ☎ WORK

FAX   BIRTHDAY

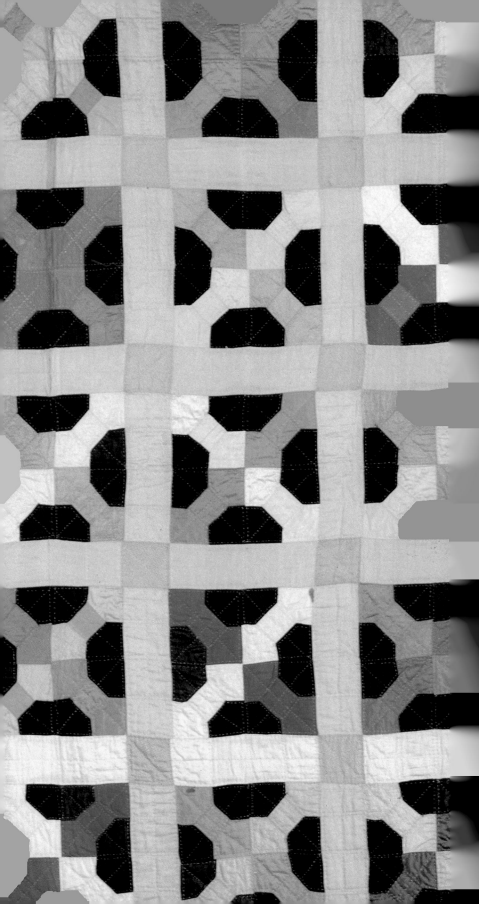

NAME	
ADDRESS	
☎ HOME	☎ WORK
FAX	BIRTHDAY
NAME	
ADDRESS	
☎ HOME	☎ WORK
FAX	BIRTHDAY
NAME	
ADDRESS	
☎ HOME	☎ WORK
FAX	BIRTHDAY
NAME	
ADDRESS	
☎ HOME	☎ WORK
FAX	BIRTHDAY
NAME	
ADDRESS	
☎ HOME	☎ WORK
FAX	BIRTHDAY

NAME

ADDRESS

☎ HOME   ☎ WORK

FAX   BIRTHDAY

NAME

ADDRESS

☎ HOME   ☎ WORK

FAX   BIRTHDAY

NAME

ADDRESS

☎ HOME   ☎ WORK

FAX   BIRTHDAY

NAME

ADDRESS

☎ HOME   ☎ WORK

FAX   BIRTHDAY

NAME

ADDRESS

☎ HOME   ☎ WORK

FAX   BIRTHDAY

NAME

ADDRESS

☎ HOME   ☎ WORK

FAX   BIRTHDAY

NAME

ADDRESS

☎ HOME   ☎ WORK

FAX   BIRTHDAY

NAME

ADDRESS

☎ HOME   ☎ WORK

FAX   BIRTHDAY

NAME

ADDRESS

☎ HOME   ☎ WORK

FAX   BIRTHDAY

NAME

ADDRESS

☎ HOME   ☎ WORK

FAX   BIRTHDAY

NAME

ADDRESS

☎ HOME   ☎ WORK

FAX   BIRTHDAY

NAME

ADDRESS

☎ HOME   ☎ WORK

FAX   BIRTHDAY

NAME

ADDRESS

☎ HOME   ☎ WORK

FAX   BIRTHDAY

NAME

ADDRESS

☎ HOME   ☎ WORK

FAX   BIRTHDAY

NAME

ADDRESS

☎ HOME   ☎ WORK

FAX   BIRTHDAY

NAME

ADDRESS

☎ HOME   ☎ WORK

FAX   BIRTHDAY

NAME

ADDRESS

☎ HOME   ☎ WORK

FAX   BIRTHDAY

NAME

ADDRESS

☎ HOME   ☎ WORK

FAX   BIRTHDAY

NAME

ADDRESS

☎ HOME   ☎ WORK

FAX   BIRTHDAY

NAME

ADDRESS

☎ HOME   ☎ WORK

FAX   BIRTHDAY

NAME

ADDRESS

☎ HOME   ☎ WORK

FAX   BIRTHDAY

NAME

ADDRESS

☎ HOME   ☎ WORK

FAX   BIRTHDAY

NAME

ADDRESS

☎ HOME   ☎ WORK

FAX   BIRTHDAY

NAME

ADDRESS

☎ HOME   ☎ WORK

FAX   BIRTHDAY

NAME

ADDRESS

☎ HOME   ☎ WORK

FAX   BIRTHDAY

NAME	
ADDRESS	
☎ HOME	☎ WORK
FAX	BIRTHDAY
NAME	
ADDRESS	
☎ HOME	☎ WORK
FAX	BIRTHDAY
NAME	
ADDRESS	
☎ HOME	☎ WORK
FAX	BIRTHDAY
NAME	
ADDRESS	
☎ HOME	☎ WORK
FAX	BIRTHDAY
NAME	
ADDRESS	
☎ HOME	☎ WORK
FAX	BIRTHDAY

NAME

ADDRESS

☎ HOME   ☎ WORK

FAX   BIRTHDAY

NAME

ADDRESS

☎ HOME   ☎ WORK

FAX   BIRTHDAY

NAME

ADDRESS

☎ HOME   ☎ WORK

FAX   BIRTHDAY

NAME

ADDRESS

☎ HOME   ☎ WORK

FAX   BIRTHDAY

NAME

ADDRESS

☎ HOME   ☎ WORK

FAX   BIRTHDAY

NAME

ADDRESS

☎ HOME   ☎ WORK

FAX   BIRTHDAY

NAME

ADDRESS

☎ HOME   ☎ WORK

FAX   BIRTHDAY

NAME

ADDRESS

☎ HOME   ☎ WORK

FAX   BIRTHDAY

NAME

ADDRESS

☎ HOME   ☎ WORK

FAX   BIRTHDAY

NAME

ADDRESS

☎ HOME   ☎ WORK

FAX   BIRTHDAY

NAME

ADDRESS

☎ HOME   ☎ WORK

FAX   BIRTHDAY

NAME

ADDRESS

☎ HOME   ☎ WORK

FAX   BIRTHDAY

NAME

ADDRESS

☎ HOME   ☎ WORK

FAX   BIRTHDAY

NAME

ADDRESS

☎ HOME   ☎ WORK

FAX   BIRTHDAY

NAME

ADDRESS

☎ HOME   ☎ WORK

FAX   BIRTHDAY

NAME

ADDRESS

☎ HOME   ☎ WORK

FAX   BIRTHDAY

NAME

ADDRESS

☎ HOME   ☎ WORK

FAX   BIRTHDAY

NAME

ADDRESS

☎ HOME   ☎ WORK

FAX   BIRTHDAY

NAME

ADDRESS

☎ HOME   ☎ WORK

FAX   BIRTHDAY

NAME

ADDRESS

☎ HOME   ☎ WORK

FAX   BIRTHDAY

NAME

ADDRESS

☎ HOME   ☎ WORK

FAX   BIRTHDAY

NAME

ADDRESS

☎ HOME   ☎ WORK

FAX   BIRTHDAY

NAME

ADDRESS

☎ HOME   ☎ WORK

FAX   BIRTHDAY

NAME

ADDRESS

☎ HOME   ☎ WORK

FAX   BIRTHDAY

NAME

ADDRESS

☎ HOME   ☎ WORK

FAX   BIRTHDAY

NAME

ADDRESS

☎ HOME   ☎ WORK

FAX   BIRTHDAY

NAME

ADDRESS

☎ HOME   ☎ WORK

FAX   BIRTHDAY

NAME

ADDRESS

☎ HOME   ☎ WORK

FAX   BIRTHDAY

NAME

ADDRESS

☎ HOME   ☎ WORK

FAX   BIRTHDAY

NAME

ADDRESS

☎ HOME   ☎ WORK

FAX   BIRTHDAY

NAME

ADDRESS

☎ HOME   ☎ WORK

FAX   BIRTHDAY

NAME

ADDRESS

☎ HOME   ☎ WORK

FAX   BIRTHDAY

NAME

ADDRESS

☎ HOME   ☎ WORK

FAX   BIRTHDAY

NAME

ADDRESS

☎ HOME   ☎ WORK

FAX   BIRTHDAY

NAME

ADDRESS

☎ HOME   ☎ WORK

FAX   BIRTHDAY

NAME

ADDRESS

☎ HOME   ☎ WORK

FAX   BIRTHDAY

NAME

ADDRESS

☎ HOME   ☎ WORK

FAX   BIRTHDAY

NAME

ADDRESS

☎ HOME   ☎ WORK

FAX   BIRTHDAY

NAME

ADDRESS

☎ HOME   ☎ WORK

FAX   BIRTHDAY

NAME

ADDRESS

☎ HOME   ☎ WORK

FAX   BIRTHDAY

NAME

ADDRESS

☎ HOME   ☎ WORK

FAX   BIRTHDAY

NAME

ADDRESS

☎ HOME   ☎ WORK

FAX   BIRTHDAY

NAME

ADDRESS

☎ HOME   ☎ WORK

FAX   BIRTHDAY

NAME

ADDRESS

☎ HOME   ☎ WORK

FAX   BIRTHDAY

NAME

ADDRESS

☎ HOME   ☎ WORK

FAX   BIRTHDAY

NAME	
ADDRESS	
☎ HOME	☎ WORK
FAX	BIRTHDAY
NAME	
ADDRESS	
☎ HOME	☎ WORK
FAX	BIRTHDAY
NAME	
ADDRESS	
☎ HOME	☎ WORK
FAX	BIRTHDAY
NAME	
ADDRESS	
☎ HOME	☎ WORK
FAX	BIRTHDAY
NAME	
ADDRESS	
☎ HOME	☎ WORK
FAX	BIRTHDAY

NAME

ADDRESS

☎ HOME   ☎ WORK

FAX   BIRTHDAY

NAME

ADDRESS

☎ HOME   ☎ WORK

FAX   BIRTHDAY

NAME

ADDRESS

☎ HOME   ☎ WORK

FAX   BIRTHDAY

NAME

ADDRESS

☎ HOME   ☎ WORK

FAX   BIRTHDAY

NAME

ADDRESS

☎ HOME   ☎ WORK

FAX   BIRTHDAY

NAME

ADDRESS

☎ HOME   ☎ WORK

FAX   BIRTHDAY

NAME

ADDRESS

☎ HOME   ☎ WORK

FAX   BIRTHDAY

NAME

ADDRESS

☎ HOME   ☎ WORK

FAX   BIRTHDAY

NAME

ADDRESS

☎ HOME   ☎ WORK

FAX   BIRTHDAY

NAME

ADDRESS

☎ HOME   ☎ WORK

FAX   BIRTHDAY

NAME

ADDRESS

☎ HOME   ☎ WORK

FAX   BIRTHDAY

NAME

ADDRESS

☎ HOME   ☎ WORK

FAX   BIRTHDAY

NAME

ADDRESS

☎ HOME   ☎ WORK

FAX   BIRTHDAY

NAME

ADDRESS

☎ HOME   ☎ WORK

FAX   BIRTHDAY

NAME

ADDRESS

☎ HOME   ☎ WORK

FAX   BIRTHDAY

NAME

ADDRESS

☎ HOME   ☎ WORK

FAX   BIRTHDAY

NAME

ADDRESS

☎ HOME   ☎ WORK

FAX   BIRTHDAY

NAME

ADDRESS

☎ HOME   ☎ WORK

FAX   BIRTHDAY

NAME

ADDRESS

☎ HOME   ☎ WORK

FAX   BIRTHDAY

NAME

ADDRESS

☎ HOME   ☎ WORK

FAX   BIRTHDAY

NAME

ADDRESS

☎ HOME   ☎ WORK

FAX   BIRTHDAY

NAME

ADDRESS

☎ HOME   ☎ WORK

FAX   BIRTHDAY

NAME

ADDRESS

☎ HOME   ☎ WORK

FAX   BIRTHDAY

NAME

ADDRESS

☎ HOME   ☎ WORK

FAX   BIRTHDAY

NAME

ADDRESS

☎ HOME   ☎ WORK

FAX   BIRTHDAY

NAME

ADDRESS

☎ HOME ☎ WORK

FAX BIRTHDAY

NAME

ADDRESS

☎ HOME ☎ WORK

FAX BIRTHDAY

NAME

ADDRESS

☎ HOME ☎ WORK

FAX BIRTHDAY

NAME

ADDRESS

☎ HOME ☎ WORK

FAX BIRTHDAY

NAME

ADDRESS

☎ HOME ☎ WORK

FAX BIRTHDAY

NAME

ADDRESS

☎ HOME   ☎ WORK

FAX   BIRTHDAY

NAME

ADDRESS

☎ HOME   ☎ WORK

FAX   BIRTHDAY

NAME

ADDRESS

☎ HOME   ☎ WORK

FAX   BIRTHDAY

NAME

ADDRESS

☎ HOME   ☎ WORK

FAX   BIRTHDAY

NAME

ADDRESS

☎ HOME   ☎ WORK

FAX   BIRTHDAY

NAME

ADDRESS

☎ HOME   ☎ WORK

FAX   BIRTHDAY

NAME

ADDRESS

☎ HOME   ☎ WORK

FAX   BIRTHDAY

NAME

ADDRESS

☎ HOME   ☎ WORK

FAX   BIRTHDAY

NAME

ADDRESS

☎ HOME   ☎ WORK

FAX   BIRTHDAY

NAME

ADDRESS

☎ HOME   ☎ WORK

FAX   BIRTHDAY

NAME

ADDRESS

☎ HOME   ☎ WORK

FAX   BIRTHDAY

NAME

ADDRESS

☎ HOME   ☎ WORK

FAX   BIRTHDAY

NAME

ADDRESS

☎ HOME   ☎ WORK

FAX   BIRTHDAY

NAME

ADDRESS

☎ HOME   ☎ WORK

FAX   BIRTHDAY

NAME

ADDRESS

☎ HOME   ☎ WORK

FAX   BIRTHDAY

NAME

ADDRESS

☎ HOME   ☎ WORK

FAX   BIRTHDAY

NAME

ADDRESS

☎ HOME   ☎ WORK

FAX   BIRTHDAY

NAME

ADDRESS

☎ HOME   ☎ WORK

FAX   BIRTHDAY

NAME

ADDRESS

☎ HOME   ☎ WORK

FAX   BIRTHDAY

NAME

ADDRESS

☎ HOME   ☎ WORK

FAX   BIRTHDAY

NAME

ADDRESS

☎ HOME   ☎ WORK

FAX   BIRTHDAY

NAME

ADDRESS

☎ HOME   ☎ WORK

FAX   BIRTHDAY

NAME

ADDRESS

☎ HOME   ☎ WORK

FAX   BIRTHDAY

NAME

ADDRESS

☎ HOME   ☎ WORK

FAX   BIRTHDAY

NAME

ADDRESS

☎ HOME   ☎ WORK

FAX   BIRTHDAY

NAME

ADDRESS

☎ HOME   ☎ WORK

FAX   BIRTHDAY

NAME

ADDRESS

☎ HOME   ☎ WORK

FAX   BIRTHDAY

NAME

ADDRESS

☎ HOME   ☎ WORK

FAX   BIRTHDAY

NAME

ADDRESS

☎ HOME   ☎ WORK

FAX   BIRTHDAY

NAME

ADDRESS

☎ HOME   ☎ WORK

FAX   BIRTHDAY

NAME

ADDRESS

☎ HOME   ☎ WORK

FAX   BIRTHDAY

NAME

ADDRESS

☎ HOME   ☎ WORK

FAX   BIRTHDAY

NAME

ADDRESS

☎ HOME   ☎ WORK

FAX   BIRTHDAY

NAME

ADDRESS

☎ HOME   ☎ WORK

FAX   BIRTHDAY

NAME

ADDRESS

☎ HOME   ☎ WORK

FAX   BIRTHDAY

NAME

ADDRESS

☎ HOME   ☎ WORK

FAX   BIRTHDAY

NAME

ADDRESS

☎ HOME   ☎ WORK

FAX   BIRTHDAY

NAME

ADDRESS

☎ HOME   ☎ WORK

FAX   BIRTHDAY

NAME

ADDRESS

☎ HOME   ☎ WORK

FAX   BIRTHDAY

NAME

ADDRESS

☎ HOME   ☎ WORK

FAX   BIRTHDAY

NAME

ADDRESS

☎ HOME   ☎ WORK

FAX   BIRTHDAY

NAME

ADDRESS

☎ HOME   ☎ WORK

FAX   BIRTHDAY

NAME

ADDRESS

☎ HOME   ☎ WORK

FAX   BIRTHDAY

NAME

ADDRESS

☎ HOME   ☎ WORK

FAX   BIRTHDAY

NAME

ADDRESS

☎ HOME   ☎ WORK

FAX   BIRTHDAY

NAME

ADDRESS

☎ HOME   ☎ WORK

FAX   BIRTHDAY

NAME

ADDRESS

☎ HOME   ☎ WORK

FAX   BIRTHDAY

NAME

ADDRESS

☎ HOME   ☎ WORK

FAX   BIRTHDAY

NAME

ADDRESS

☎ HOME   ☎ WORK

FAX   BIRTHDAY

NAME

ADDRESS

☎ HOME   ☎ WORK

FAX   BIRTHDAY

NAME

ADDRESS

☎ HOME   ☎ WORK

FAX   BIRTHDAY

NAME

ADDRESS

☎ HOME   ☎ WORK

FAX   BIRTHDAY

NAME

ADDRESS

☎ HOME   ☎ WORK

FAX   BIRTHDAY

NAME

ADDRESS

☎ HOME   ☎ WORK

FAX   BIRTHDAY

NAME

ADDRESS

☎ HOME   ☎ WORK

FAX   BIRTHDAY

NAME

ADDRESS

☎ HOME   ☎ WORK

FAX   BIRTHDAY

NAME

ADDRESS

☎ HOME   ☎ WORK

FAX   BIRTHDAY

NAME

ADDRESS

☎ HOME   ☎ WORK

FAX   BIRTHDAY

NAME

ADDRESS

☎ HOME   ☎ WORK

FAX   BIRTHDAY

NAME

ADDRESS

☎ HOME   ☎ WORK

FAX   BIRTHDAY

NAME

ADDRESS

☎ HOME   ☎ WORK

FAX   BIRTHDAY

NAME

ADDRESS

☎ HOME   ☎ WORK

FAX   BIRTHDAY

NAME

ADDRESS

☎ HOME   ☎ WORK

FAX   BIRTHDAY

NAME

ADDRESS

☎ HOME   ☎ WORK

FAX   BIRTHDAY

NAME

ADDRESS

☎ HOME   ☎ WORK

FAX   BIRTHDAY

NAME

ADDRESS

☎ HOME   ☎ WORK

FAX   BIRTHDAY

NAME

ADDRESS

☎ HOME   ☎ WORK

FAX   BIRTHDAY

NAME

ADDRESS

☎ HOME   ☎ WORK

FAX   BIRTHDAY

NAME

ADDRESS

☎ HOME   ☎ WORK

FAX   BIRTHDAY

NAME

ADDRESS

☎ HOME   ☎ WORK

FAX   BIRTHDAY

NAME

ADDRESS

☎ HOME   ☎ WORK

FAX   BIRTHDAY

NAME

ADDRESS

☎ HOME   ☎ WORK

FAX   BIRTHDAY

NAME

ADDRESS

☎ HOME   ☎ WORK

FAX   BIRTHDAY

NAME

ADDRESS

☎ HOME   ☎ WORK

FAX   BIRTHDAY

NAME

ADDRESS

☎ HOME   ☎ WORK

FAX   BIRTHDAY

NAME

ADDRESS

☎ HOME   ☎ WORK

FAX   BIRTHDAY

NAME

ADDRESS

☎ HOME   ☎ WORK

FAX   BIRTHDAY

NAME

ADDRESS

☎ HOME   ☎ WORK

FAX   BIRTHDAY

NAME

ADDRESS

☎ HOME   ☎ WORK

FAX   BIRTHDAY

NAME

ADDRESS

☎ HOME   ☎ WORK

FAX   BIRTHDAY

NAME

ADDRESS

☎ HOME   ☎ WORK

FAX   BIRTHDAY

NAME

ADDRESS

☎ HOME   ☎ WORK

FAX   BIRTHDAY

NAME

ADDRESS

☎ HOME   ☎ WORK

FAX   BIRTHDAY

NAME

ADDRESS

☎ HOME   ☎ WORK

FAX   BIRTHDAY

NAME

ADDRESS

☎ HOME   ☎ WORK

FAX   BIRTHDAY

NAME

ADDRESS

☎ HOME   ☎ WORK

FAX   BIRTHDAY

NAME

ADDRESS

☎ HOME   ☎ WORK

FAX   BIRTHDAY

NAME

ADDRESS

☎ HOME   ☎ WORK

FAX   BIRTHDAY

NAME

ADDRESS

☎ HOME   ☎ WORK

FAX   BIRTHDAY

NAME

ADDRESS

☎ HOME   ☎ WORK

FAX   BIRTHDAY

NAME

ADDRESS

☎ HOME   ☎ WORK

FAX   BIRTHDAY

NAME

ADDRESS

☎ HOME   ☎ WORK

FAX   BIRTHDAY

NAME

ADDRESS

☎ HOME   ☎ WORK

FAX   BIRTHDAY

NAME

ADDRESS

☎ HOME   ☎ WORK

FAX   BIRTHDAY

NAME

ADDRESS

☎ HOME   ☎ WORK

FAX   BIRTHDAY

NAME

ADDRESS

☎ HOME   ☎ WORK

FAX   BIRTHDAY

NAME

ADDRESS

☎ HOME   ☎ WORK

FAX   BIRTHDAY

NAME

ADDRESS

☎ HOME   ☎ WORK

FAX   BIRTHDAY

NAME

ADDRESS

☎ HOME   ☎ WORK

FAX   BIRTHDAY

NAME

ADDRESS

☎ HOME   ☎ WORK

FAX   BIRTHDAY

NAME

ADDRESS

☎ HOME   ☎ WORK

FAX   BIRTHDAY

NAME

ADDRESS

☎ HOME   ☎ WORK

FAX   BIRTHDAY

NAME

ADDRESS

☎ HOME   ☎ WORK

FAX   BIRTHDAY

NAME

ADDRESS

☎ HOME   ☎ WORK

FAX   BIRTHDAY

NAME

ADDRESS

☎ HOME   ☎ WORK

FAX   BIRTHDAY

NAME

ADDRESS

☎ HOME   ☎ WORK

FAX   BIRTHDAY

NAME

ADDRESS

☎ HOME   ☎ WORK

FAX   BIRTHDAY

NAME

ADDRESS

☎ HOME   ☎ WORK

FAX   BIRTHDAY

NAME

ADDRESS

☎ HOME   ☎ WORK

FAX   BIRTHDAY

NAME

ADDRESS

☎ HOME   ☎ WORK

FAX   BIRTHDAY

NAME

ADDRESS

☎ HOME   ☎ WORK

FAX   BIRTHDAY

NAME

ADDRESS

☎ HOME   ☎ WORK

FAX   BIRTHDAY

NAME

ADDRESS

☎ HOME   ☎ WORK

FAX   BIRTHDAY

NAME

ADDRESS

☎ HOME   ☎ WORK

FAX   BIRTHDAY

NAME

ADDRESS

☎ HOME   ☎ WORK

FAX   BIRTHDAY

NAME

ADDRESS

☎ HOME   ☎ WORK

FAX   BIRTHDAY

NAME

ADDRESS

☎ HOME   ☎ WORK

FAX   BIRTHDAY

NAME

ADDRESS

☎ HOME   ☎ WORK

FAX   BIRTHDAY

NAME

ADDRESS

☎ HOME   ☎ WORK

FAX   BIRTHDAY

NAME

ADDRESS

☎ HOME   ☎ WORK

FAX   BIRTHDAY

NAME	
ADDRESS	
☎ HOME	☎ WORK
FAX	BIRTHDAY
NAME	
ADDRESS	
☎ HOME	☎ WORK
FAX	BIRTHDAY
NAME	
ADDRESS	
☎ HOME	☎ WORK
FAX	BIRTHDAY
NAME	
ADDRESS	
☎ HOME	☎ WORK
FAX	BIRTHDAY
NAME	
ADDRESS	
☎ HOME	☎ WORK
FAX	BIRTHDAY

NAME

ADDRESS

☎ HOME   ☎ WORK

FAX   BIRTHDAY

NAME

ADDRESS

☎ HOME   ☎ WORK

FAX   BIRTHDAY

NAME

ADDRESS

☎ HOME   ☎ WORK

FAX   BIRTHDAY

NAME

ADDRESS

☎ HOME   ☎ WORK

FAX   BIRTHDAY

NAME

ADDRESS

☎ HOME   ☎ WORK

FAX   BIRTHDAY

NAME

ADDRESS

☎ HOME   ☎ WORK

FAX   BIRTHDAY

NAME

ADDRESS

☎ HOME   ☎ WORK

FAX   BIRTHDAY

NAME

ADDRESS

☎ HOME   ☎ WORK

FAX   BIRTHDAY

NAME

ADDRESS

☎ HOME   ☎ WORK

FAX   BIRTHDAY

NAME

ADDRESS

☎ HOME   ☎ WORK

FAX   BIRTHDAY

NAME

ADDRESS

☎ HOME   ☎ WORK

FAX   BIRTHDAY

NAME

ADDRESS

☎ HOME   ☎ WORK

FAX   BIRTHDAY

NAME

ADDRESS

☎ HOME   ☎ WORK

FAX   BIRTHDAY

NAME

ADDRESS

☎ HOME   ☎ WORK

FAX   BIRTHDAY

NAME

ADDRESS

☎ HOME   ☎ WORK

FAX   BIRTHDAY

NAME	
ADDRESS	
☎ HOME	☎ WORK
FAX	BIRTHDAY
NAME	
ADDRESS	
☎ HOME	☎ WORK
FAX	BIRTHDAY
NAME	
ADDRESS	
☎ HOME	☎ WORK
FAX	BIRTHDAY
NAME	
ADDRESS	
☎ HOME	☎ WORK
FAX	BIRTHDAY
NAME	
ADDRESS	
☎ HOME	☎ WORK
FAX	BIRTHDAY

NAME

ADDRESS

☎ HOME   ☎ WORK

FAX   BIRTHDAY

NAME

ADDRESS

☎ HOME   ☎ WORK

FAX   BIRTHDAY

NAME

ADDRESS

☎ HOME   ☎ WORK

FAX   BIRTHDAY

NAME

ADDRESS

☎ HOME   ☎ WORK

FAX   BIRTHDAY

NAME

ADDRESS

☎ HOME   ☎ WORK

FAX   BIRTHDAY

IMPORTANT NUMBERS